WILDERNESS SELF RELIANCE

It is much better to have more knowledge and less kit than the other way around. There are a few items that are essential. If you find yourself in a survival situation, you may need to be able to create some basic tools and weapons in order to survive.

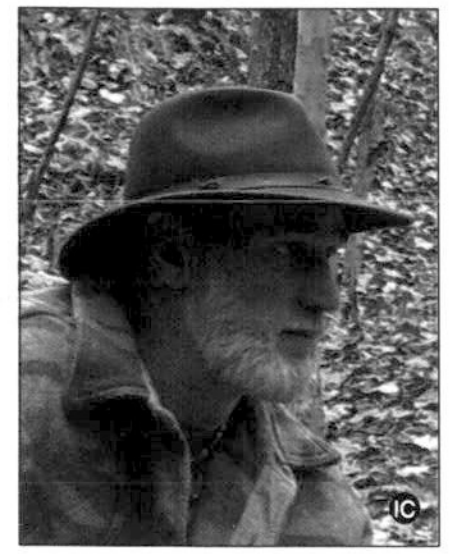

My Pathfinder Outdoor Survival Guides offer you the most simple and common sense approach to being prepared for a survival situation. If you practice the skills and techniques that are discussed in these guides, you will be in a far superior position when the situation arises.

Most important is that you develop the ability to adapt, improvise and overcome adversity by learning to use what is available to you, and that you stay firm in your belief that you CAN survive – never give up.

The Pathfinder School System®

Created as a teaching tool for my students in Wilderness Self Reliance, the Pathfinder School System represents the wisdom of the ancient scouts who ventured ahead of nomadic tribes to find fresh areas to support their community.

These "Pathfinders" had to accurately identify the perfect spot to sustain their tribes – they had to recognize the resources that would afford food, shelter, water, medicines and protection – the very same resources a person would need today.

This system is designed to introduce you to the knowledge you need to increase your survivability.

Before You Go

Plan – Be sure someone knows where you are going, when you should return, and have a commitment from them to establish search & rescue if you don't report on time. Make this a habit – we don't plan to get lost, and once you are lost, it is too late to plan.

Be knowledgeable – Study your environment. Your ability to find water, build a shelter, make fire and find food will be greatly enhanced by a familiarity with terrain, vegetation and climate.

Be equipped – Build and practice the use of your survival kit components. The kit contents that I advocate save you the most exertion and make the most difference to your survivability. **Don't just buy them – practice using them.** Master their use before you head into the wilderness.

Dave Canterbury is a master woodsman with over 20 years of experience working in many dangerous environments. He has taught survival and survival methods to hundreds of students and professionals in the US and around the world. His common sense approach to survivability is recognized as one of the most effective systems of teaching known today. For information on Pathfinder programs and materials visit http://www.thepathfinderschoolllc.com.

N.B. – The publisher makes no representation or warranties with respect to the accuracy, completeness, correctness or usefulness of this information and specifically disclaims any implied warranties of fitness for a particular purpose. The advice, strategies and/or techniques contained herein may not be suitable for all individuals. The publisher shall not be responsible for any physical harm (up to and including death), loss of profit or other commercial damage. The publisher assumes no liability brought or instituted by individuals or organizations arising out of or relating in any way to the application and/or use of the information, advice and strategies contained herein.

Made in the USA

Waterford Press produces reference guides that introduce novices to nature, science, survival and outdoor recreation. Product information is featured on the website: **www.waterfordpress.com.**

Text and illustrations © 2012, 2020 by Waterford Press Inc. All rights reserved. Images marked IC © Iris Canterbury 2012, 2020. For permissions, or to share comments, e-mail editor@waterfordpress.com.

To order or for information on custom-published products, call 800-434-2555 or e-mail info@waterfordpress.com.

ISBN 978-1-58355-711-2 $7.95 U.S.

UPC

10 9 8 7 6 5 4 3 2 1 203601

IMPROVISED HUNTING WEAPONS – A Waterproof Folding Guide to Making Simple Tools for Survival

PATHFINDER OUTDOOR SURVIVAL GUIDE™

IMPROVISED HUNTING WEAPONS

A Waterproof Folding Guide to Making Simple Tools for Survival

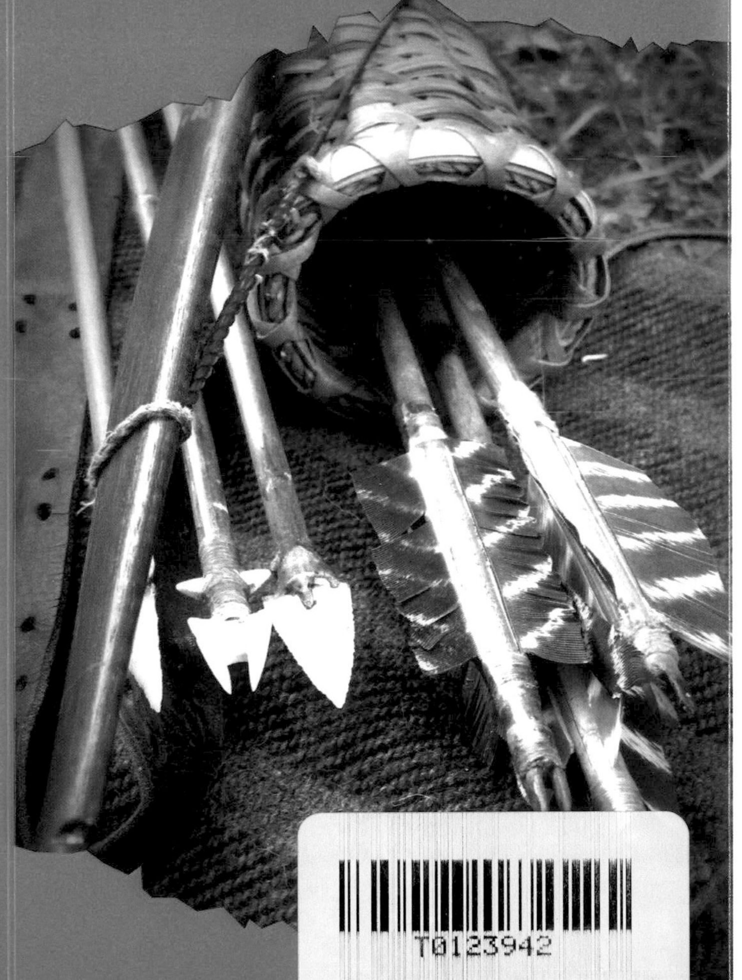

THE PATHFINDER SCHOOL

www.thepathfinderschoolllc.com

TOOL THEORY

Improvised tools and weapons will improve your chances in a survival situation. The essentials when you are considering which tools to build are the same as the basics for survivability: what will give you the greatest return for your investment?

You need a cutting device, cordage — with which you can build other tools or traps—and fire, used to harden your tools or cook any food that you kill. Your second line tools include those that can be fashioned with little exertion from materials found in the wild: a throwing stick (Rabbit Stick) that can be found in a simple branch or piece of wood, a sling fashioned from your bandana, or a walking stick that doubles as a spear. All of these will offer strong returns for minimal investment if you understand the basics of their construction and uses.

If longer term survival is at stake, or if the food you need requires more aggressive tools, then you will have to construct more complex traps and weapons as the need arises. In all cases, knowing how to use the tool is as important as being able to build it. As with your survival kit basics, practice building and using these tools before you are in a survival situation so you can respond when the need arises.

BUILDING A CUTTING BLADE

If you are without a knife, one of the first primitive tools you must build is a knife or cutting tool. If you are lucky, you will find a tin with a sharp edge, or a bone that you can hone to a fine edge. If not those, you may need to look at creating a blade or cutting edge out of stone. The most common stone for making a blade is a quartz-like stone (quartzite or agate will flake the best).

To make a primitive blade with rock, these are the basic steps:

Find a stone of the type that will flake but retain a hard edge when broken (you may need to 'test drop' a few stones to establish the character of the rock. Once you find one, this will be your 'blank', to be shaped into a blade.

Find a second stone of heavier material, suitable for holding in one hand, but shaped in such a way that you can control the striking point against your blank. (To avoid destroying your blank, and more importantly, to avoid crushing your fingers on the hand that is holding the blank).

Try to cushion the blank so the striking rock doesn't shatter it (either on a rolled up shirt or other softening materials) laid on a stone. You are unlikely to be able to hold the blank in one hand and hit it with a stone in the other hand – best to rest the blank on a surface and then concentrate on holding the striking stone at the correct angle to chip/flake away layers on the sharpening edge of the blank. Your blows should be in the direction in which the flake should run – if the blank is hit downward at a 90 degree angle, the flakes will come off short and stubby, which isn't a good shape for a cutting tool.

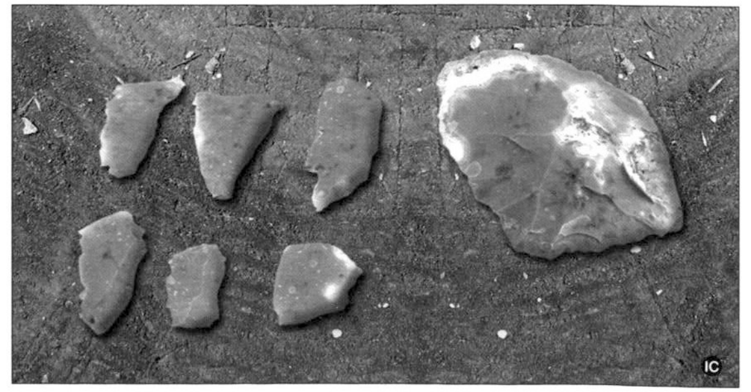

SIMPLE THROWING WEAPONS

Rabbit Stick

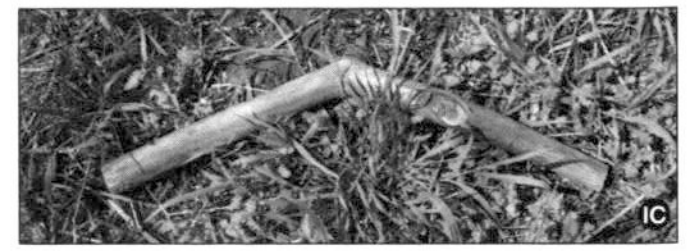

A rabbit stick or throwing stick is a simple but ingenious device that takes little energy to produce, and which can pay big dividends toward securing game. These hunting tools were used for thousands of years and take only a little practice to become accurate. Thrown side arm at a low angle, the rabbit stick is a very effective small game weapon. It can be created with no tools if necessary by simply breaking off a branch.

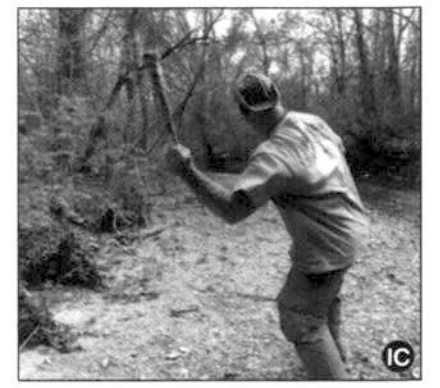

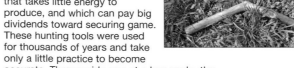

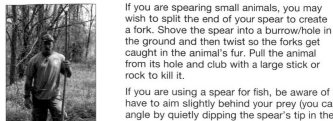

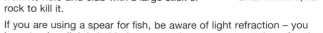

The rabbit stick is a very useful tool and should be one of the first you make once survival priorities of shelter, water, and fire are finished. With this tool you can effectively take game, use it as a digging stick, as well as baton your knife to process wood or take down small trees.

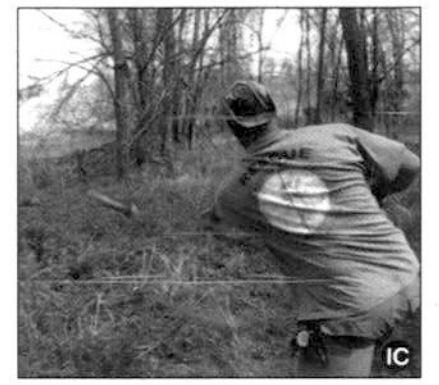

To fashion this tool, find a branch approximately the same diameter as your wrist. It should be made of hard wood about the length of your arm from armpit to palm. It can be curved or straight. This weapon often resembles a one-ended Australian boomerang, and is thrown sidearm to strike the animal with blunt force. You can increase its effectiveness by carving both ends to a point and fire hardening them.

Hold the long end, opposite to the 'elbow', to throw. Because it is long, it has a larger margin of error than a simple rock thrown at game.

Rocks

Use fist-sized stones to stun an animal (aim at its head and shoulder area). Have a large stick or a large rock handy to use for the final kill, and move in quickly once you have hit the animal so it does not recover and escape.

Sling

A simple sling made from your bandana, folded in half with a rock tucked inside, will work to hurl rocks at game. This takes a bit of practice but again takes little energy to create.

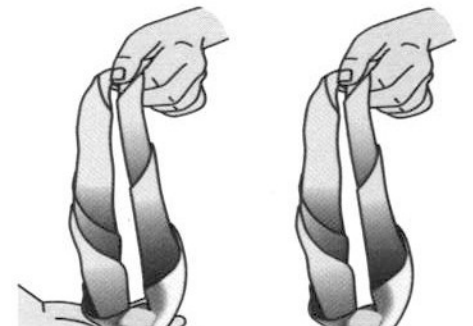

Bola

A bola is a multi-stringed weapon with rocks that is thrown at animals to entangle their legs. To make one, take three lengths of paracord or bank line (about 2 feet each), and tie them to rocks about the size of a girl's fist (about ½ lb. each). Tie the other end of the strings together into a single knot.

To throw the bola, hold it by the knotted end and twirl the lines and rocks over your head or out to your side until they are spinning at a good, controlled speed, then direct your hand toward your prey and release the bola. Have a 'kill stick' or rock at the ready so you can dispatch your prey quickly.

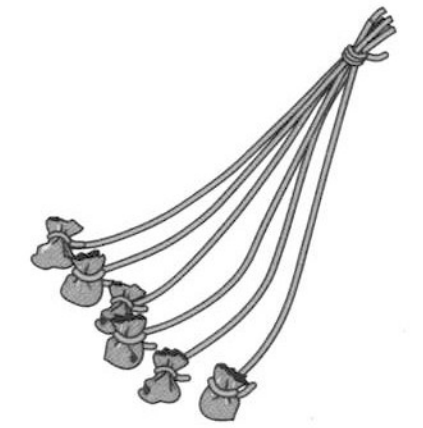

You can also place the stones in small 'bags' of fabric or plastic and tie these to the line.

MULTI-USE SPEARS

Long Spear/Walking Stick

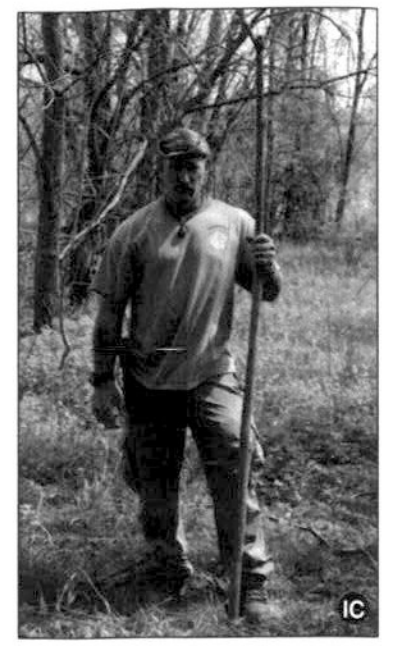

Walking in areas where footing is uncertain is hazardous. This is compounded if you are tired and hungry. A good walking stick with opposite ends adapted to be a fork and spear gives you a multi-functional survival tool, and it takes very little energy to produce.

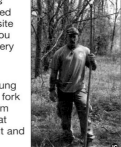

Start with a hardwood stick, at least 2" in diameter and 6" taller than you are. Cut a young sapling if you can. The ideal stick will have a fork at one end (where it forms two branches). Trim the forked end to leave about a 6" fork with at least two tines, carve the other end to a point and harden both ends over fire if possible.

Note that the forked end should be used for stability in walking and for pinning down game. The pointed end atop can be fashioned into a frog or fish gig if desired later but better to make a separate tool for this altogether and have both.

This tool will give you a walking stick to help with footing, cross-stream, and a tool to flush out snakes from suspected areas and a spear to pin an animal. This tool will also make a good reliable digging stick to secure roots and tubers as well as digging for insect grubs and worms for food or bait. It can also be used as a support for your shelter if necessary.

Throwing Spear

If you have to try to catch game with a throwing spear, make one that is between 5 and 6 feet long with a sharpened point at one end. The spear should be as long as you are tall.

To throw it, hold the spear parallel to the ground above shoulder height with your dominant hand. Position your hand at the center of the spear's length or where it is evenly balanced end to end. Stand with your foot opposite to your throwing hand forward for balance, and then throw with a strong thrust aimed at the animal's chest/heart area.

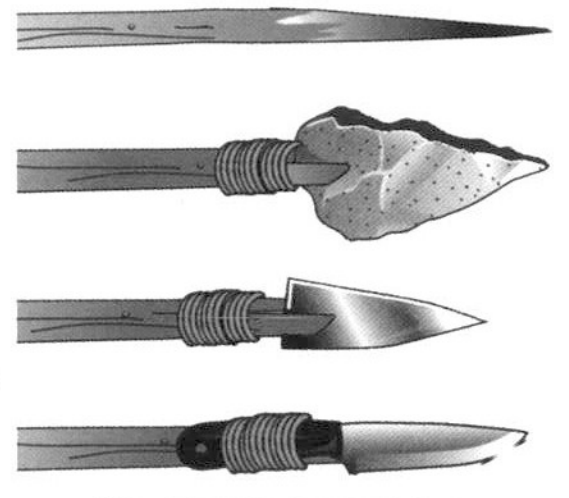

The simplest spear is a pointed stick that has the tip tempered by fire. You can make spear points from a variety of materials including a stone flake, a flattened triangle of tin or a knife.

Tracking Stick

Another use for your spear is to make an impromptu tracking stick. This is as simple as making marks on the stick or using moveable cordage that is wrapped up and down the stick to measure the distance in an animal's stride.

To measure stride, establish the length of one full stride from the animal's front foot to its opposite back foot, then place the end of your spear in the center of the rear track, move the loop or mark your stick in the center of the front track. Once this is complete, you can place the stick in any track and determine where the next track should fall within a reasonable arc of your mark on the stick. This technique comes in handy if trailing an animal over rough ground or where prints are not necessarily made or visible with every step.

TIP Make your walking stick longer than you are tall so you don't accidentally impale yourself if you trip and fall with it.

DIRECT CONTACT WEAPONS

Small Animal Spears

If you are spearing small animals, you may wish to split the end of your spear to create a fork. Shove the spear into a burrow/hole in the ground and then twist so the forks get caught in the animal's fur. Pull the animal from its hole and club with a large stick or rock to kill it.

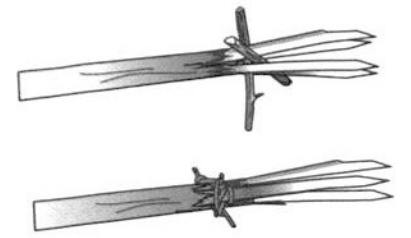

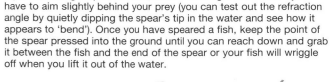

Small Animal Spear

If you are using a spear for fish, be aware of light refraction – you have to aim slightly behind your prey (you can test out the refraction angle by quietly dipping the spear's tip in the water and see how it appears to 'bend'). Once you have speared a fish, keep the point of the spear pressed into the ground until you can reach down and grab it between the fish and the end of the spear or your fish will wriggle off when you lift it out of the water.

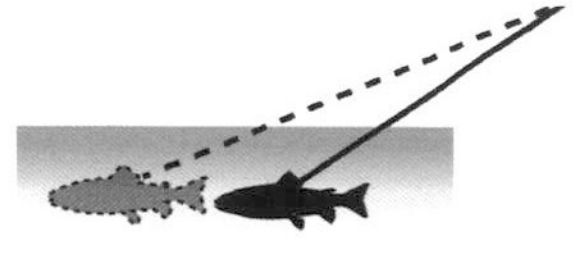

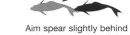

You will see the fish ahead of where it actually is.

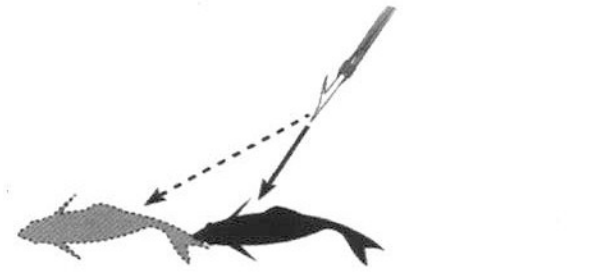

Aim spear slightly behind where you see the fish.

Noose/Lasso on Spear

This is an effective way of pulling roosting birds out of trees. Slip the noose over the bird and then tighten the noose and pull the bird out of the tree at the same time.

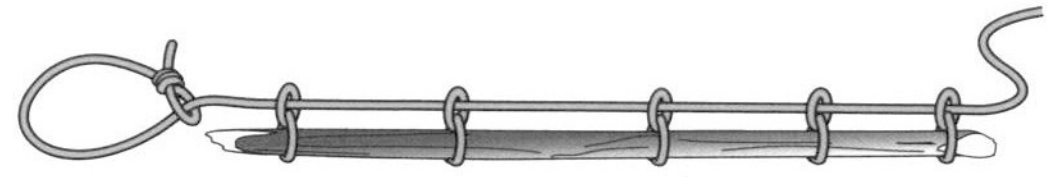

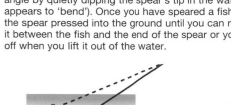

USEFUL TOOL & WEAPON KNOTS

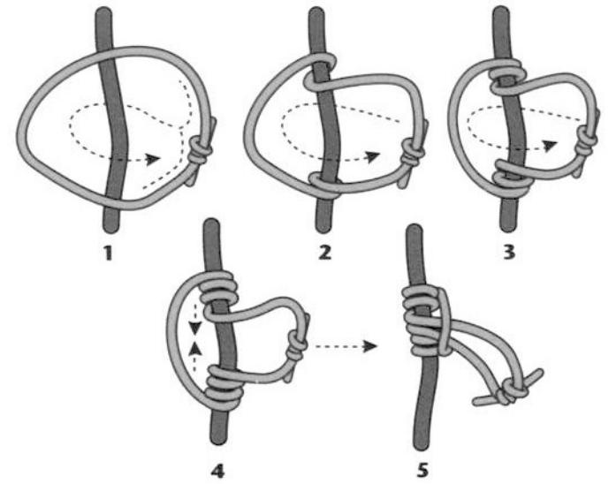

Prusik Knot
Used for gill nets and dip nets

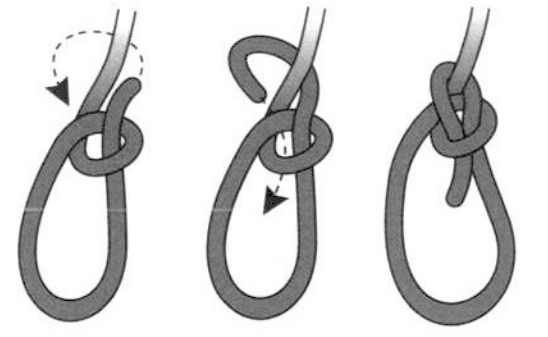

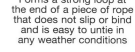

Bowline
Forms a strong loop at the end of a piece of rope that does not slip or bind and is easy to untie in any weather conditions

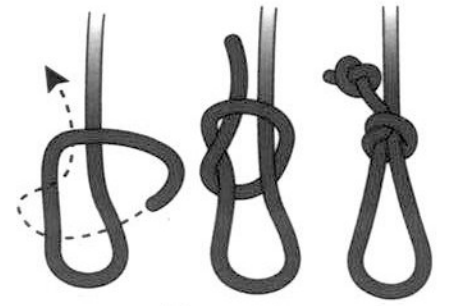

Noose
Running loop used in snares

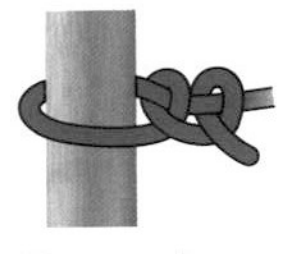

Two and a Half Hitches
Used to attach bowstring to bow

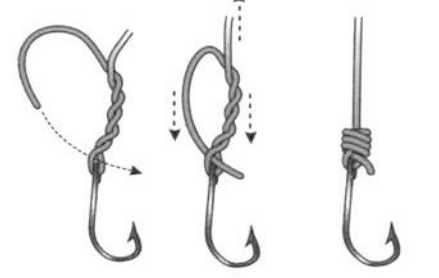

Improved Clinch Knot
Used to attach lures to fishing line

Bow & Arrow

The bow and arrow has been used for centuries. In a survival situation, where you have no other means of killing food, consider making a bow and arrow. You will need a strong, flexible branch at least 5 feet long and about 1"-2" in diameter (not more than 2" before you peel it). Notch it at both ends (about 2" from the ends) to allow cord to be tied and then tightened to form the bow. Ideally, you want wood with a straight grain, no knots, and lots of fresh growth to ensure its flexibility (a dry, older branch will just break).

This bow is made from straight sticks (10 or so) of fairly uniform thickness that are bound together into a bundle, tapered towards both ends by staggering the sticks, which are then tied/bound together (from the center) in such a way as to achieve the taper.

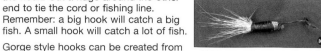

From the middle working out, layer the sticks in alternate shapes, overlapping in the center. When you pick the bundle up in the center, your hand should just fit around the diameter (if it doesn't, add or remove sticks to accomplish this). Use paracord or fishing line to wrap the boughs together in the center. Remember, you're not trying to make this perfect, just useable.

Create a loop toward the end of your wrap and tighten your wrap around it to secure the loop (it might be handy later). End your wrap with square knots. Now you're going to move down the bow, drop down about 6" or 8" from the top, and start wrapping up to the top of the bow. Again, add a loop as you complete the wrap. (Once you've done middle, top, and bottom, you'll have three wraps on the bow.) Do the corresponding wrap on the bottom end.

The bow should be about as long as your outreached arm span, so if it is longer, you need to cut it down. However, leave one stick about an inch longer than the rest at either end, to attach the bow string. You will now make your final wrap at the top and bottom (you will have a total of five wraps). You will attach your bow line to the highest post and step into it like you would a normal bow and pull over it to draw. There's your strung bow.

The bowstring can be any of a number of materials. Ideally, you have paracord or bank line. If not, then you will need to find suitable material to make a string. Ancients used sinew or rawhide strips – if you have stumbled over a carcass, then you can attempt to harvest sinew or just strip the hide and cut strips about 1/8" wide as long as you can get, in quantities that can be twisted into a bowstring (finished length will need to be about 6 ft.).

Temper Tools with Fire

To temper tools and weapons on fire, pull out some coals to one side, and allow them to cool to a glow. Lay the arrow/spear point or other tool over the coals and heat slowly, turning to avoid allowing the wood to catch fire or burn deeper than the surface layer. Pull the spear away from the fire at regular intervals and rub the wood to harden the heated surface. Stop heating the wood when it is fully blackened and you have rubbed a smooth hard surface on the tempered end.

The quality of your arrow will determine your success in bow hunting. Depending on what is available, you can make an arrow shaft using small saplings or light, straight branches from any of these species: birch, willow, maple, oak, ash, bamboo, dogwood, serviceberry or hickory.

The length of your arrow depends on your draw (how far back you will pull the bowstring); arrows are generally about 3 ft. long and about 3/8" in diameter. Sharpen the "arrow" end to a fine point, harden in fire if possible. Cut a notch in the back end of the arrow – wrap just behind the nock to keep it solid when held on the bow-string. If available, use feathers as the "fletching" or Duct Tape to help the arrow travel straight once shot. If you have nothing to create fletching, then your arrow should be made of wood that is light-weight and pithy inside (river cane, willow or bamboo best). Arrows will need to be weight forward in design to fly true, tapering the shaft or using the smaller end for the nock will help with this. Many things can be fashioned into arrow heads in an emergency to make them more effective, from soda can metal to broken glass. Arrows can be straightened by heating over a fire and bending until cool.

Slingshot/Slingshot Bands

This is one of the most effective small game gathering devices you can use for the energy spent. You need to have a stretchable band for this tool. Any heavy "Y" branch will create a solid frame and parachute cord will secure the bands. Ammunition is as plentiful as rocks on the ground. A slingshot is not difficult to become efficient with, and adds little weight compared to its food gathering capabilities. Proper slingshot form is much like archery form, and a well-aimed rock from one of these can be devastating to small and medium size game animals.

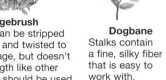

Many of us played with slingshots as kids, like any other weapon, takes practice to be accurate.

To make a blade from bone, you need to prepare the bone prior to striking it or shaping it. If you have found a long bone from the limb of an animal, you will need to split it and then sharpen the edges of one end as a cutting tool. To split a bone without shattering it, you need to 'score' or 'engrave' a line down one side with a sharp rock edge, then turn the bone over and do the same

to the reverse. Then, tap it with a small stone along the "engraved" score line on both sides until it cracks. Once you have the split bone, use another rock to abrade or grind the bone edge until it forms a sharp edge.

If not rock or bone, then a blade from a sharpened piece of hardwood is the next option. Using an abrasive rock, file the wood to a sharp point or file one side of the wood to a sharp edge to work as a cutting tool.

Fish Hooks from Wood, Tin or Bone

Needles, safety pins, wire or any small piece of metal can be formed into fish-hooks. Or you can take a small piece of hardwood (about 1" long, about 1/8th inch thick) and carve a hook – make a notch about 1/3 of the length from one end and carve back into the wood to form the hook. Cut a ridge around the other end to tie the cord or fishing line. Remember: a big hook will catch a big fish. A small hook will catch a lot of fish.

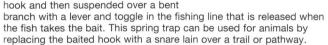

Gorge style hooks can be created from hardwood slivers which are just pointed on both ends like a toggle. These are tied off center to pivot when the hook is set.

This image shows a single ply of bank line used with a natural locust thorn and deer hair to make an effective fishing fly.

Gill Net from Cordage or Bank Line

You can make a net from lengths of bank line or paracord. The size of the net will be determined by your materials and what you intend to catch in the net. Finer mesh will take more line, but will catch a range of sizes of fish and animals. Start by tying a length of cord between two trees. This will be an edge of your net when finished. Now tie a number of core lines to the suspension line (the number of core lines defines the mesh size. Use a Prusik knot or girth hitch to tie the core lines to the suspension line.

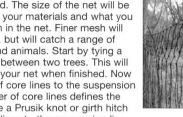

Starting at one end, tie the first and third line, and then the second and fourth line, and so on to create the first layer of knots/mesh web. Return down the line tying the alternating cords in another series to create the diamond shapes, back and forth until you have used up your cord lengths and created a mesh net. Once ready, position your net in a waterway (weight the bottom with rocks to hold it on the bottom, stretch it across a stream or river tied to a vine or branch).

This net is multi-functional. Make sure to funnel the fish into this net if not long enough to stretch the width of the waterway. You can travel up stream and drive fish to the net by throwing rocks or walking down stream. If the mesh is small enough you can also fashion this into a dip net or trap by use of hoops made from green saplings.

Pocket Fishing Kit

Fish and frogs are probably the easiest meat sources to secure. A simple fishing kit will greatly increase your odds of success, and are fun to practice with when you are in the outdoors. Make a kit with a small canister (or use a section of PVC pipe with one end sealed and a cap on the other end. On the outside, wrap about 50 yards of 50# spider wire. This line is small enough in diameter to secure small fish, but will hold a 'big boy' if you catch one. All other components can fit inside of the canister, and should include: five each of #6 and #8 hooks; several split shot; a couple of small bobbers; 12 inches of red yarn.

NOTE: Red is a good color for attracting both fish and frogs. A hook with a bit of red yarn dangled in front of a resting frog will almost always catch it.

Fish Traps

You can make a **fish basket** by tying several sticks into a funnel shape with vines or palm fronds. After creating a funnel shape tie some barbs facing into the funnel made of hardwood to poke the fish and keep him from backing out of the trap baited at the small end of the funnel. Place the trap with the opening on the upstream side and anchor it to the bottom with stakes.

The fish spring trap is a land-based system that releases in a springing action under tension. Fishing line or thin cordage is hung over a bent sapling or tied to a bungee; you anchor the line using a Y-shaped branch as the base of the trap. The other end is tied to a baited hook and then suspended over a bent branch with a lever and toggle in the fishing line that is released when the fish takes the bait. This spring trap can be used for animals by replacing the baited hook with a snare lain over a trail or pathway.

Dip Net

Dip nets can be used to scoop small fishes, tadpoles and insects from the water. Can be fashioned from cordage, t-shirts or bandannas.

If you are without paracord or bank line in your survival kit, or if you have lost your survival kit, then after a cutting device, you will need to make cordage to aid in the construction of your improvised hunting weapons, as well as for shelter and possibly for self-rescue.

The fibrous plants you should look for include those with pithy stalks such as dogbane, milkweed, wild hemp and fireweed. You should be able to pull long strips of the stems to form your cordage basis. Non-pithy plants such as stinging nettles and sagebrush should be pounded, using a rounded stone against a wood log, to soften but not break the stalks. Wet the fibers if you need to, in order to make them workable, and then wind or braid the strands to the length you need. Often, cordage from plant matter is stronger when wet.

Prepare fiber by pounding dry stems to remove woody parts, then clean the remaining fiber by hand, peeling out lengths of fiber and laying them to dry, then braid, twine or twist them the way a person spinning wool does to form long threads. Lengths are extended by adding in and twisting new pieces. Double and triple the first cordage lengths in a similar twining motion to create stronger rope.

Braid bundles of fibers to make cordage

These are the plants most suitable for cordage materials

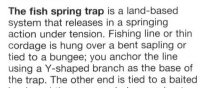

Stinging Nettle
Stalks contain strong fiber than can be used for fishing line, bow strings, snares, nets, ropes and even mending threads.

Sagebrush
Dry bark can be stripped from trunk and twisted to form cordage, but doesn't have strength like other plants and should be used for binding rather than weight-bearing purposes.

Dogbane
Stalks contain a fine, silky fiber that is easy to work with.

Poplar
Use strips of inner white bark to make cordage (it is stronger when wet or damp).

Milkweed
Stalks contain a silky material. This plant can be used whether plant is green or dry.

In addition to these plants, the inner bark of trees can also be used. The best trees for this purpose are hickory, poplar, basswood, elm, walnut, aspen, cottonwood, maple or cedar.

Find a tree with dead bark; strip off long sections of the fibrous inside (cambium) layer. If the inner strips are hard to separate from the bark, soak the strips in heated water until the fibers come apart. If you have to use a green tree, try to take only a few thin strips from it. If you strip too much, it will kill the tree.

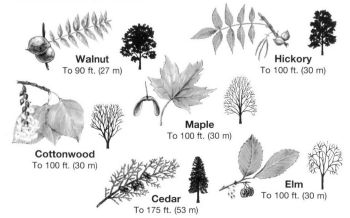

Walnut To 90 ft. (27 m)

Hickory To 100 ft. (30 m)

Cottonwood To 100 ft. (30 m)

Maple To 100 ft. (30 m)

Cedar To 175 ft. (53 m)

Elm To 100 ft. (30 m)

TIP The roots of spruce and other conifers are also good cordage resources.

It is unlikely that you have a clean environment for dressing any game you kill in a survival situation, so these are the basics you need to know to avoid making yourself sick through poor butchering or handling techniques.

1. **Ensure the animal is dead** – Prod it with a stick. Have a weapon handy to finish the job in case it is not.

2. **Gut the animal as soon as possible** – It is important to get the intestines and stomach out of the body quickly so they don't spoil the meat. Avoid puncturing the guts or stomach of all animals to avoid contamination.

3. **Clean the body cavity as best you can** – Use your hands, a bandana or leaves to wipe out the body cavity. Keep the meat out of direct sunlight if possible, or get it over a flame to cook to avoid it from spoiling.

4. **Clean your hands as best you can** – This will prevent you from accidentally ingesting inedible parts.

5. **Retain inedible parts for bait** – Save this bait away from your campsite if there is a risk of attracting predators.

1. **Never kill**, handle or consume any animal that appears slow, sluggish or sick.

2. **Don't handle or consume** brains, spinal tissues or eyeballs.

3. **On larger animals**, remove the meat from bones and cook it thoroughly.

4. **Rabbits** carry the disease tularemia, which can often be detected by the presence of a white-spotted liver. Cook rabbits until very well done to kill the germ.

5. **Organ meats** – heart, liver and kidneys – should be inspected for signs of worms or other parasites. The liver should be a deep red or purple color and have a smooth, wet surface.

6. **Many animals die from natural causes**, many do not, it is good to be wary of animals found dead, due to the fact that they may have been killed by another animal that carried Rabies and rabies can be transferred through saliva on the carcass.

1. **Knife** – avoid using your knife if you have other effective weapon choices to avoid damaging or losing it. If needed, it can be thrown at prey or strapped to a spear handle.

2. **Combustion Device** – fire will harden spear ends and cook your catch.

3. **Cover** – can create a blind to hide you from prey. Puncture with small holes to make a dip net.

4. **Cordage** – binding for weapons and trap components.

5. **Cargo Tape** – binding for weapons and traps if no cordage.

6. **Cotton Bandana** – used as sling, binding and dip net.

7. **NOTE:** Found materials such as an old tin can, broken glass and other discarded trash are invaluable for improvised weapons – don't walk past anything that might be incorporated into a weapon or tool, even if you can't see a use for it at the time.

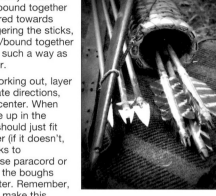